HOW TO RECEIVE YOUR HEALING

But He was wounded for our transgressions, He was bruised for our iniquities; The chastisement for our peace was upon Him, And by His stripes we are healed.
—Isaiah 53:5

TED SHUTTLESWORTH

Unless otherwise indicated, all Scripture quotations are from the King James Version of the Bible.

How to Receive Your Healing
ISBN 978-1-7336042-4-6

www.tedshuttlesworth.com

Published by T.S.E.A., Inc.
Post Office Box 7
Farmington, West Virginia 26571
USA

Cover design by Ted Shuttlesworth Jr.

Printed in the United States of America

CONTENTS

INTRODUCTION

There is a biblical road that you must travel to receive healing from the Lord. It is a journey from sickness to health.

There are many hurting people who have never heard the oldest story of help and healing. It is the oldest story because it is based on He who is Alpha.

It is the last word on healing no matter how many modern cures remain yet to be discovered, for He is Omega. The beginning of your journey to health and the end of your healing quest is found in the person of Jesus Christ!

> **I am Alpha Omega, the beginning and the ending, saith the Lord, which is, and which was, and which is to come, the Almighty.**
>
> **Revelation 1:8**

Isaiah looked through God's telescope and saw through the ages to come. He saw the One *"which is, and which was, and which is to come..." (Revelation 1:8)* This same prophet wrote:

> **But he was wounded for our transgression, he was bruised for our iniquities: the chastisement of our peace was upon him; and with his stripes we are healed.**
> **Isaiah 53:4,5**

Matthew chapter eight is the healing chapter of the New Testament. It is in this chapter that the prophecy of Isaiah 53 finds its actual fulfillment. What Isaiah saw through God's telescope focused in on the human drama of suffering's meeting with Heaven's Healing Balm.

Ted Shuttlesworth Sr.
Hill Cottage, West Virginia
October, 2021

CHAPTER 1

HOW TO RECEIVE YOUR HEALING

And when Jesus was entered into Capernaum, there came unto him a centurion, beseeching him, And saying, Lord, my servant lieth at home sick of the palsy, grievously tormented. And Jesus saith unto him, I will come and heal him. The centurion answered and said, Lord, I am not worthy that thou shouldest come under my roof: but speak the word only, and my servant shall be healed. For I am a man under authority, having soldiers under me: and I say to this man, Go, and he goeth; and to another, Come, and he cometh; and to my

servant, Do this, and he doeth it. When Jesus heard it, he marvelled, and said to them that followed, Verily I say unto you, I have not found so great faith, no, not in Israel.

Matthew 8:5-10

The greatest faith comes through understanding the authority of God's Word! There is no experience that is above the Word of God. There is no sickness that is greater than the Word of God.

He sent His word, and healed them...
Psalm 107:20

The centurion recognized the authority that was in the words of Jesus. The Word of God is the vehicle that carries your healing to you. This transportation system never fails.

While traveling on the railroad from London to Gatwick airport, I saw a train that had derailed. The newspapers declared several had been killed.

They never reached their final destination. God's Word always reaches its destination and it will always accomplish that which God has intended.

> **So shall my word be that goeth forth out of my mouth: it shall not return unto me void, but it shall accomplish that which I please, and it shall prosper in the thing whereto I sent it.**
>
> **Isaiah 55:11**

The centurion knew that the beginning of his servant's healing was the Word of the Lord! All healing starts with the Word of God.

WHERE FAITH COMES FROM

> **So then faith cometh by hearing, and hearing by the word of God.**
>
> **Romans 10:17**

Where you go to church is important! What you hear preached is vital! Billy Sunday said, "Going to church no more saves you than sitting in a garage makes you a car!"

We might paraphrase that by saying; "Going to a church will no more heal you than sitting in a garage will make you a car!"

Your church or your pastor may not believe in divine healing. Since everything we receive from God is based upon faith, it does make a difference where you go to church and what you hear preached. Separate yourself from unbelief.

> **Having a form of godliness, but denying the power thereof: from such turn away.**
>
> **2 Timothy 3:5**

Years ago, I had erected a tent in one of the greater cities of America. Night by night, God performed wonderful miracles when we prayed in the name of Jesus.

One night in particular, they brought to me a young boy born deaf and dumb. They call them deaf mutes. My father-in-law stood by my side and we agreed that God would perform the miracle.

I commanded the deaf and dumb spirits to go and never return, in the name of Jesus. Instantly, that boy heard and began to make sounds for the first time in his life. It was a wonderful miracle. I instructed the parents to teach him how to speak. Our hearts were thrilled for them.

I had that tent up for almost two weeks. On Sundays we encouraged the people to go to their own churches and I preached for the sponsoring church.

The Monday night after the first weekend, a woman

approached me and my wife as we drove up behind the tent. I recognized her as the woman who had brought the boy who had been deaf and dumb. She told me a story that I have never forgotten.

Apparently, when the parents went to their church on Sunday, they told the pastor of the great miracle that God had done. When the pastor heard it he replied.

"God did not heal your boy in that tent!"

"No, he is healed, pastor, come see," they told him. But that pastor would not believe.

Later, during the service, he told the congregation that God was not performing miracles in that tent meeting and he forbid his people to attend the next week. (Completely ignoring the young boy who sat in the service.)

The mother then told us that the same pastor was out in front of the tent with a notebook writing down all the names of his people who were there that night. He was going to throw them out of his church if they came.

The mother told us one more thing that brought me great joy. She said that when they went home on Sunday, the boy let them know that when that preacher stood to preach, he could not hear one word that the minister said, even though he could hear all the other noises around him!

God certainly has a sense of humor. I am convinced that there are certain so-called "ministers" whom God does not want us to hear. I tell people, "Find a church that is red hot, where they preach the full gospel."

Many in the church world today are missing God's instruction in this area. Instead of finding others of like precious faith and fellowshipping with them, some have said, "Well, I'll just stay in my old church and try to change them."

If God has not been able to change many of these traditional churches who reject His power, what makes you think you are going to be able to change them? Separate yourself from unbelief.

The centurion was not a part of the "household of Israel," but Jesus said that his faith was the greatest in all of Israel. This was the greatest faith Jesus had ever seen.

THE GREATEST FAITH

Why did the centurion have the greatest faith Jesus had ever seen? The centurion was a soldier. Apparently, he was a compassionate man. He cared for his servant.

The Bible tells us that he showed kindness to the Jews of Capernaum. He paid for the construction of a synagogue for them. This man was not the typical oppressor of the poor. Rome ruled with a heavy hand. Yet, this man cared for his servant and with kindness, served his community through the expense of a house for God and

His people. What made his faith the greatest in all of the New Testament? HE UNDERSTOOD AUTHORITY!

> **For I am a man under authority.**
> **Matthew 8:9**

> **Where the word of the King is, there is power...**
> **Ecclesiastes 8:4**

The Word and authority are synonymous. The centurion was not the only one that recognized this authority in the words of Jesus.

> **And they were astonished at his doctrine; for his word was with power.**
> **Luke 4:32**

> **And they were all amazed, and spake among themselves, saying, what a word is this! For with authority and power he commandeth the unclean spirits, and they come out.**
> **Luke 4:36**

> **He taught them as one having author-
> ity, and not as the scribes.**
>
> **Matthew 7:29**

There are two words that are very important in understanding the difference between *"authority"* and
"power."

The word *"power"* in Luke 4:36 is the Greek word
"dunamis." It is the same word in Acts 1:8:

> **But ye shall receive power, after that the
> Holy Ghost is come upon you: and ye
> shall be witnesses unto me both in Jeru-
> salem, and in all Judaea, and in Samaria,
> and unto the uttermost part of earth.**
>
> **Acts 1:8**

Dunamis is the word from which we get the English
word, dynamite. Power! It signifies ability, might, of
mighty works and miracles.

The second word is *"authority"* in Luke 4:36. It comes
from the Greek word, *"exousia"* meaning *"the right to act."*

This was the basis of the centurion's faith. Literally,
he said, "Jesus, you have the right to make my servant
whole, just by saying so!" If that was true in that day, it
is still true today.

Jesus Christ the same yesterday, and to-day, and forever.

Hebrews 13:8

The word contains the seed for healing. When Jesus spoke, literally the word or words spoken, contained within them the right to make it happen! The centurion, who himself was a man of authority and under authority, recognized this principle in the ministry of Jesus. The centurion concluded; "If I can just get Jesus to say that my servant is healed, he will be all right!"

...but speak the word only, and my servant shall be healed.

Matthew 8:8

Jesus taught this principle to His disciples by parable:

THE PARABLE OF THE SOWER

And he taught them many things by parables, and said unto them in his doctrine. Hearken; Behold, there went out a sower to sow: And it came to pass, as he sowed, some fell by the way side, and the fowls of the air came and devoured

it up. And some fell on stony ground,
where it had not much earth; and immediately it sprang up, because it had
no depth of earth: But when the sun
was up, it was scorched; and because
it had no root, it withered away. And
some fell among thorns, and the thorns
grew up, and choked it, and it yielded
no fruit. And other fell on good ground,
and did yield fruit that sprang up and
increased; and brought forth, some thir-
ty, and some sixty, and some hundred.
And he said unto them, He that hath
ears to hear, let him hear.

Mark 4:2-9

Jesus taught in parables to "them that were without."
However, to you and I who are His disciples; "...it is
given to know the mystery of the kingdom of God."

This parable of the sower and the seed is the parable
which is the foundation to understanding all the other
parables that Christ taught.

...Know ye not this parable? and how
then will ye know all parables?

Mark 4:13

The parable of the sower, then, is the key to all parables and it is also the foundation for all healing. Freedom from sickness comes from knowing the truth. Remember this scripture?

> **Sanctify them through thy truth: thy word is truth.**
>
> **John 17:17**

The word sanctify means separate. God's Word will separate you from sin, sickness, and death.

> **And ye shall know the truth, and the truth shall make you free.**
>
> **John 8:32**

Somehow the centurion unlocked the door that brought healing. When Jesus would speak the word, that word was truth.

No matter the illness or disease of his servant, the healing word became the truth; the disease became the lie! No matter the symptoms or apparent condition, the word of authority overruled! Hallelujah! Fenton's translation of Psalm 107:20 says, *"He sent His word, and it healed them."*

THE HEALING SEED

> **Now the parable is this: The seed is the word of God.**
>
> **Luke 8:11**

A farmer will not receive a harvest until he plants a seed. The seed is powerless until it is planted. The first thing that God tells us about "seed" is in the Book of Beginnings.

> **And God said, Behold, I have given you every herb bearing seed, which is upon the face of all the earth, and every tree, in the which is the fruit of a tree yielding seed; to you it shall be for meat.**
>
> **Genesis 1:29**

God gives the seed! Isaiah records:

> **For as the rain cometh down, and the snow from heaven, and returneth not thither, but watereth the earth, and maketh it bring forth and bud, that it may give seed to the sower, and bread to the eater: So shall my word be that goeth**

forth out of my mouth:

>Isaiah 55:10,11

The seed is the Word of God! Now, here is the foundation for our healing. Here is how healing comes to our bodies. The centurion knew it and said:

>...speak the word only, and my servant
>shall be healed.
>
>>Matthew 8:8

The Word is seed. When spoken, it is planted. Preachers, you get what you preach!

>But what saith it? The word is nigh thee,
>even in thy mouth, and in thy heart: that
>is, the word of faith, which we preach;
>
>>Romans 10:8

>How then shall they call on him in
>whom they have not believed? and how
>shall they believe in him of whom they
>have not heard? and how shall they
>hear without a preacher?
>
>>Romans 10:14

**So then faith cometh by hearing, and
hearing by the word of God.**

Romans 10:17

Faith for healing comes by hearing the Word for healing. Preach salvation! People will be saved. Preach the baptism of the Holy Ghost! People will receive the Holy Ghost. Preach healing! People will be healed!

God said that the seed contains its ability inside itself. There are seeds that will bring forth corn because that seed is a corn seed or kernel.

**And God said, let the earth bring forth
grass, the herb yielding seed, and the
fruit tree yielding fruit after his kind,
whose seed is in itself, upon the earth:
and it was so.**

Genesis 1:11

When you hear a healing message, you are allowing a *"healing seed"* to be planted in your spirit. It will bring forth healing. These seeds of plants and herbs were already finished before they were in the ground.

**...in the day that the Lord God made the
earth and the heavens, And every plant**

of the field before it was in the earth, and every herb of the field before it grew:

Genesis 2:4,5

Healing belongs to you, even before it is planted in your heart. Jesus has already carried your sickness and borne your affliction.

...Himself took our infirmities and bare our sicknesses.

Matthew 8:17

There is no sickness greater than the Word of God. All healing begins with the Word of God. (Romans 10:17.) Separate yourself from unbelief! (II Timothy 3:5.)

God's Word is the greatest authority! Freedom from sickness comes from knowing the truth. (John 8:32.) Your *"healing seeds"* are the Scriptures on healing. (Luke 8:11.)

Remember, Jesus does not have less authority today to heal you than He did then. If He could speak authoritative words of healing then, His words of authority can heal you NOW!

CHAPTER 2

IF GOD IS SO GOOD, WHY DO PEOPLE SUFFER?

Why am I sick? How can I get well? Why am I suffering? Did I do something wrong that brought sickness upon me? Is God punishing me?

The age-old question that many have asked is "If God is so good, then why do people suffer? God is omnipotent. He is all powerful, and all He would have to do is intervene and stop all the suffering in the world.

It is not wrong to think these thoughts or to wonder why things seemingly are going wrong in your life.

> Come now, and LET US REASON TO-GETHER, saith the Lord: though your sins be as scarlet, they shall be as white as snow; though they be red like crim-

son, they shall be as wool.

Isaiah 1:18

Your answer to these questions and more are always found in the Word of God. The Lord wants us to be able to give an answer to everyone concerning their salvation, health and healing and general well-being.

MY CRISIS OF FAITH

The Outer Banks of North Carolina bring tourists from all over the world. Albemarle and the Pamlico Sounds are grounds for many of the fishermen who work to make a living there.

The Gulf Stream is just fourteen miles southeast of Cape Hatteras. This beautiful paradise is where I experienced my greatest crisis of faith.

A fisherman was attending our meeting at the Buxton Assembly of God. He and his wife came to the altar and gave their hearts to the Lord. They approached me one night and asked if I would go and pray for their baby at the Children's Hospital in Norfolk, Virginia.

I drove to Norfolk and went into the hospital. They directed me to the children's ward where the baby was. I told the head nurse at the ward station why I was there: I had come to pray for the child.

Another nurse came to lead me through the ward and as I walked away, I heard the head nurse say to the other ladies, "If God is so good then why are these little children suffering."

I did not have an answer that day, but since then, the Lord has given me the answer that I want to share with you.

I returned home from the hospital to my parents' home in Virginia Beach. My mom fixed me lunch before I was to return to the church in the Outer Banks.

After lunch, I went into the den to rest, but my mind was troubled from the words that the nurse had spoken. How could I stand to minister to people if God would only help some of them? Why were all those children sick? Then, the Lord spoke to me.

The wind came down the chimney and stirred the ashes and the embers in the fireplace began to glow. Suddenly, three verses of scripture came to my mind. They were in this order:

> **Every good gift and every perfect gift is from above, and cometh down from the Father of lights, with whom is no variableness, neither shadow of turning.**
>
> **James 1:17**

> The thief cometh not, but for to steal, and to kill, and to destroy: I am come that they might have life, and that they might have it more abundantly.
>
> John 10:10

> How art thou fallen from heaven, O Lucifer, son of the morning! how art thou cut down to the ground, which didst weaken the nations!
>
> Isaiah 14:12

THE GOODNESS OF GOD

Healing is a revelation of the character and nature of God. God is the giver of good gifts (James 1:17). He is a God of love.

> Beloved, let us love one another: for love is of God; and every one that loveth is born of God, and knoweth God. He that loveth not knoweth not God; for GOD IS LOVE.
>
> 1 John 4:7, 8

The more you read the Bible, the more you will understand that He is also a good God. He is absolutely good, all the time. The Lord revealed Himself to Moses in the book of Exodus.

> **And he said, I will make all my GOOD-NESS pass before thee, and I will proclaim the name of the Lord before thee; and will be gracious to whom I will be gracious, and will shew mercy on whom I will shew mercy.**
>
> **Exodus 33:19**

When God shows up, something good is going to happen! King David understood this when he said, *"Surely GOODNESS and mercy shall follow me all the days of my life: and I will dwell in the house of the Lord forever."* *Psalm 23:6*

The Psalmist echoes this wonderful truth of God's nature in the following verse which is repeated four times in Psalm 107.

> **Oh that men would praise the Lord for his goodness, and for his wonderful works to the children of men!**
>
> **Psalm 107:8,15,21,31**

The prophet Hosea reminded the children of Israel, *"Afterward shall the children of Israel return, and seek the Lord their God, and David their king; and shall fear the Lord and HIS GOODNESS in the latter days." Hosea 3:5*

God's nature is such that He will not go back on His Word. God is good and His promises are good.

> **Blessed be the Lord, that hath given rest unto his people Israel, according to all that he promised: THERE HATH NOT FAILED ONE WORD OF ALL HIS GOOD PROMISE, which he promised by the hand of Moses his servant.**
>
> **1 Kings 8:56**

When we look at all of the healing promises that the Lord gave to Moses, it is an encouragement to our faith to know not one word of His promise will fail!

The Lord established His covenant of healing when He spoke to Moses at the bitter waters of Marah. It was here that the Lord revealed to Moses that He was "The Lord that healeth thee" (Exodus 15:26).

One of the redemptive names of God is given in this scripture, Jehovah-Rapha. "I am the Lord your Physician" or "The Lord that Healeth Thee." This was the very first promise that God gave His children after He brought them out of Egypt. He told them that it was a "statute" or a law of healing.

It is interesting to me that from the time God gave this promise, to the time of the writing of the book of Kings, this healing promise was still working. It had not failed.

One preacher declared, "God will turn this old world upside-down before He will allow one of His promises to fail." There are healing promises in every book of the Bible. God wants you well spiritually, emotionally, and physically.

The greatest revelation of the goodness of God is seen in Jesus Christ. The ministry of healing is seen as a manifestation of good.

> **How God anointed Jesus of Nazareth with the Holy Ghost and with power: who went about DOING GOOD, and healing all that were oppressed of the devil; for God was with him.**
>
> **Acts 10:38**

Healing is a good thing. God heals because of His nature and provides promises for your healing that will never fail.

> For ALL THE PROMISES OF GOD IN
> HIM ARE YEA, and in him Amen, unto
> the glory of God by us.
>
> **2 Corinthians 1:20**

The Lord does not say "no" or "maybe" to His promises. The Bible declares that He says "YES" to your healing. Praise God!

My wife and I were driving to a meeting and I turned the radio on to listen to a Christian radio station. A minister was teaching on the promises of God. He said something that aggravated my spirit.

"Folks, sometimes God says no to His promises. He is sovereign and does what He wants." Sovereignty simply means that God does what He wills. The Word of God is the will of God revealed. It is His Word which reveals His sovereignty.

He said, "YES" to His law of healing and He will not go back on His Word. The Word of God is our bedrock foundation for a faith that cannot be moved or shaken by the storms of life that come against us.

THE NATURE OF SICKNESS AND DISEASE

Sickness is not a good gift. The laws that are governing the Earth came into being with the fall of man.

> **Wherefore, as by one man SIN EN-TERED INTO THE WORLD, AND DEATH BY SIN; and so death passed upon all men, for that all have sinned:**
>
> **Romans 5:12**

The law of sin and death came into existence when Adam opened the door through his disobedience. Adam and Eve believed the serpent's word, which was a lie!

> **And the serpent said unto the woman, YOU SHALL NOT SURELY DIE:**
>
> **Genesis 3:4**

Satan had taken the form of the serpent (Revelation 12:9) and challenged God's Word. His words were a lie! When Adam and Eve acted on these words, it defiled humanity with a lie. Therefore sin and death are founded on the words of the devil. The devil is a liar! Sickness is based on a lie. If you are not healed of sickness it can lead to death.

Healing is based on truth. It is the truth of God's Word.

Satan used words to bring sin, sickness, and death.

God uses His word to bring healing and life!

Satan is seen as the defiler of mankind. He seeks the ultimate destruction of all humanity. Jesus came to destroy the works of Satan.

> **He that committeth sin is of the devil; for the devil sinneth from the beginning. For this purpose the Son of God was manifested, that he might destroy THE WORKS OF THE DEVIL.**
>
> **1 John 3:8**

Jesus Christ is seen destroying the works of the devil in the four Gospels and through the Holy Spirit in the book of Acts.

1. Sickness is an oppression of the devil.

> **How God anointed Jesus of Nazareth with the Holy Ghost and with power: who went about doing good, and HEALING ALL THAT WERE OPPRESSED OF THE DEVIL; for God was with him.**
>
> **Acts 10:38**

2. Sickness is a binding spirit.

> And, behold, there was a woman which
> had a SPIRIT OF INFIRMITY eighteen
> years, and was bowed together, and
> could in no wise lift up herself. And
> when Jesus saw her, he called her to
> him, and said unto her, Woman, thou
> art loosed from thine infirmity. And he
> laid his hands on her: and immediately
> she was made straight, and glorified
> God.
>
> **Luke 13:11-13**

3. Sickness can bring death.

> For he longed after you all, and was full
> of heaviness, because that ye had heard
> that he had been sick. For indeed he
> was SICK NIGH UNTO DEATH..."
>
> **Philippians 2:26, 27**

When you compare the nature of sickness and disease to the power of healing, you find Satan is in di-
rect opposition to Christ; which brings me to the second
scripture the Lord gave to me so many years ago.

The thief cometh not, but for to steal, and to kill, and to destroy: I am come that they might have life, and that they might have it more abundantly.

John 10:10

It was the devil attacking those little children. He tries to steal your best years of life, kill your dreams of a long life, and ultimately destroy your life altogether.

Get it straight. Jesus taught us that the thief steals, kills, and destroys. The ONLY purpose that the thief, that devil, comes for is to attack you. He does not come to give, bring life, or restore. The Apostle Paul wrote to the church in Rome:

FOR SIN SHALL NOT HAVE DOMIN-ION OVER YOU: for ye are not under the law, but under grace"

Romans 6:14

If sin, which came into being when Adam fell, cannot have dominion over you, then sickness cannot have dominion over you. They both came from the same source — Satan.

SICKNESS COMES FROM SATAN

The last verse that the Lord gave me that afternoon in my parents' home is found in the Old Testament.

> **How art thou fallen from heaven, O Lucifer, son of the morning! how art thou cut down to the ground, which didst WEAKEN THE NATIONS!"**
>
> **Isaiah 14:12**

The phrase "weaken" can also be translated, "make sick." *Strong's Hebrew Concordance* gives us the Hebrew word *"challah"* which means "to be weak or sick." This passage reads in the original language that the "son of the morning . . . made the people sick."

What was the one thing that Lucifer wanted and can never have? The answer is found in *Isaiah 14:14 "I will ascend above the heights of the clouds; I will be LIKE the most High."*

He wanted to have or be made into the likeness or image of God. The Lord simply said no to his prideful boast and threw him out of heaven.

Jesus said, *"And he said unto them, I beheld Satan as lightning fall from heaven." (Luke 10:18)* God had another plan which included YOU!

And God said, Let us make man in our image, after our likeness:

Genesis 1:26

Every time Satan sees you, it reminds him of what he can never be. We are created in the image and likeness of God. Therefore he works to steal, kill and destroy that image through wars, famines, earthquakes, plagues, and sickness. (Matthew 24:7.)

In ancient times, a signet ring was used by royalty to certify that the bearer of a letter represented the king. Wax would be poured upon the parchment, and then the king would press his ring into the wax leaving a seal that represented him.

That is exactly what God did when He created you. We have that divine imprimatur stamped upon our bodies and we represent the image and likeness of God.

We have been given royal authority to bring the message the good news of who Jesus is and what He can do.

"Have you ever heard the story,
How our Lord before He died.
Laid His blessed hands in healing
Upon all who to Him cried?

How the sick and all oppressed ones,

He rejoicing sent away.
Oh I'm so glad, so glad to tell you,
He is just the same today!"

—Selected

CHAPTER 3

GOD WANTS YOU TO BE HEALED

When he was come down from the mountain, great multitudes followed him. And, behold, there came a leper and worshipped him, saying, Lord, if thou wilt, thou canst make me clean. And Jesus put forth his hand, and touched him, saying, I will; be thou clean. And immediately his leprosy was cleansed.

Matthew 8:1-3

Jesus is always ready and willing to touch the untouchable. The leper risked his life to find the answer to this question. *"Is it your will, Jesus, for lepers to be healed?"*

Faith for healing begins with God's Word. The leper was listening for Jesus' word. Yes, meant hope and health! No, meant disease and death!

Jesus said, *"I will; be thou clean." Matthew 8:3*

Two words created faith in the leper's heart.

Two words spelled the end of a lonely life.

Two words stopped the spread of a dreaded disease.

Two words ended the suffering in this man's flesh.

Two words released faith in the heart of the seeker.

"I WILL." When the "I AM" says "I WILL," all Heaven shouts while hell cries and earth is made glad!

It is never God's will for you to be sick! God is not the author of your sickness. He is not redeeming you through allowing a disease to destroy you. You are redeemed through the blood that Jesus shed for you over two thousand years ago on the old rugged Cross on Golgotha's brow!

> **But if we walk in the light, as He is in the light, we have fellowship one with another, and the blood of Jesus Christ his Son cleanseth us from all sin.**
> **1 John 1:7**

> **For all have sinned, and come short of the glory of God; Being justified freely**

> by his grace through the redemption
> that is in Christ Jesus: Whom God hath
> set forth to be a propitiation through
> faith in his blood, to declare his righ-
> teousness for the remission of sins that
> are past, through the forbearance of
> God;.
>
> **Romans 3:23-25**

FAITH IN HIS BLOOD! Faith does not come through some filthy tumor or cancer eating the life out of your flesh. God is not using some foul disease or affliction to chastise you as His child. God is not sending sickness upon this world to work out *"righteousness"* in their lives. Righteousness comes through faith in Christ's blood!

There are those who teach a *"limited atonement"* when it comes to the work of the Cross. These false teachers of religion have doomed whole generations to suffer under the guise of *"God is working out some mysterious good."*

The blood of Jesus is enough! You are not made *"more holy"* or *"more spiritual"* by disease. It is not Calvary and cancer. It is not the atonement and arthritis. It is not faith and fever!

The holy blood of Jesus, all by itself, is enough to

THEY CAME TO HEAR AND BE HEALED.
(LUKE 6:18)

cover all your sin. Faith in His blood is enough to make you righteous and give you right-standing with God. Calvary covers it all!

THE TRUE CROSS

When I was a young teenage preacher, I remember reading a book that contained an old legend of how that even the Cross that Jesus died on brought healing and deliverance.

The story was told of how the mother of one of the emperors set out on a pilgrimage to Jerusalem. When she reached that Holy City, she gave instructions to find the Cross that Jesus was crucified on.

Her men went to the foot of Golgotha and began to rummage through the piles of rubbish, in hopes of finding His Cross. They were surprised when their search revealed three crosses! However, the inscription which was placed over the head of Jesus was lying in a different place from where the crosses were.

They did not know which cross was the real Cross. They gathered together all the sick, diseased, and afflicted that they could find. They brought them to one cross and had them touch it, but nothing happened. They took them to another Cross. When they tried it, the blind eyes were opened, deaf ears came unstopped, the lame leaped for joy, the sick were made whole. They had found the true Cross!

Thank God for the Cross! God used the death of Christ to bring life to you, both spiritually and physically.

God is not the author of your sickness. If God is willing for one to be made whole of their disease, He is willing that all should be made whole. If not, then one can only assume that God has favored one over another. Yet, the Bible teaches that God is no respecter of people. He loves us all the same! Whether you are rich or poor, black or white, a man or a woman, young or old, sick or well, God loves you.

> **Then Peter opened his mouth, and said, of a truth I perceive that God is no respecter of persons:**
>
> **Acts 10:34**

> **For God so loved the world, that He gave His only begotten son, that whosoever believeth in him should not perish, but have everlasting life.**
>
> **John 3:16**

God loves humanity. He is not adding to the suffering of souls. He is not using dreaded diseases as *"love tokens"* from Heaven to *"bless"* mankind.

...for God is love. 1 John 4:8

Do not err, my beloved brethren. Every good gift and every perfect gift is from above, and cometh down from the Father of lights, with whom is no variableness, neither shadow of turning.
James 1:16,17

Sickness is not a good gift. It brings death and destruction when there is no cure. If, as some contend, that sickness can sometimes be God working out a Divine purpose, then would not those who believe such nonsense be fighting the will of God by using medicines and doctors to get well?

Would it not be better to stay sick for His glory? Then, what happens if the doctor's administrations or the medicine brings a cure? Are the natural powers of man greater than the works of God? No, God is not the author of sickness or disease, and he is not using your sickness to *"redeem"* you.

Sickness is never a work of God. The coming of Jesus was the beginning of the end of rampant destruction through sin, sickness, and death.

> ...For this purpose the son of God was manifested, that He might destroy the works of the devil.
>
> 1 John 3:8

> How God anointed Jesus of Nazareth with the Holy Ghost and with power: who went about doing good, and healing all that were oppressed of the devil; for God was with him.
>
> Acts 10:38

Jesus came to destroy the destroyer. Satan is the Apollyon (destroyer) of Revelation 9:11. Jesus said concerning this conflict of the ages:

> The thief cometh not, but for to steal, and to kill, and to destroy: I am come that they might have life, and that they might have it more abundantly.
>
> John 10:10

Here, we have the mission of Satan and the mission of the Good Shepherd revealed; death and life, robbery and abundance. Sickness is an oppression of Satan. It steals your health from you. It is Satan, the murderer, at work. It is incipient death.

Healing is God's anointing upon Jesus for all that are sick. It is the dynamic power of the Holy Ghost in explosions of deliverance. It is God with you. It is God, *"the Lord that healeth thee."* It is the Holy Ghost, the *"Paracletos,"* the One called alongside to help. It is Jesus, the Healer of humanity. Three have become one to bless and do good!

When Jesus opened the eyes of the blind, caused the deaf to hear, and made the lame to walk, the people testified that it was good.

> **And were beyond measure astonished, saying, He hath done all things well: he maketh both the deaf to hear, and the dumb to speak.**
>
> **Mark 7:37**

It is a good thing to heal the sick and make the afflicted whole. Conversely, it is a bad thing, if not an evil thing, to make people sick or afflict them. Moses declared sickness to be an evil thing!

> **...the evil diseases of Egypt.**
>
> **Deuteronomy 7:15**

James taught the early church that God does not *"tempt"* or *"test"* His children with evil.

> **Let no man say when he is tempted, I
> am tempted of God: For God cannot be
> tempted with evil, neither tempteth he
> any man.**
>
> **James 1:13**

The Bible says sickness is an evil thing. (Deuteronomy 7:15) God does not use evil to test any man. (James 1:13)

Jesus was anointed to destroy the works of the devil. (Acts 10:38; 1 John 3:8) Sickness is an oppression of the devil (Acts 10:38). The people who saw Jesus heal said the He had done well (Mark 7:37). The leper found out that it was Jesus' will for him to be made whole (Matthew 8:3). Peter taught that God is no respecter of persons.(Acts 10:34).

WHAT GOD WILL DO FOR ONE: HE WILL DO FOR ALL!

IT IS GOD'S WILL FOR YOU, TOO, TO BE WHOLE!

The first signpost on the road to healing reads. "I WILL." Make no mistake here friend. Jesus is willing to make you whole. It is the will of God for you to be healed!

Faith comes by hearing! When Jesus said, *"I will,"* the leper now had access to the miracle-working power of God. FAITH IS NOT A NATURAL FORCE! FAITH IS THE ABILITY OF GOD REVEALED! MAN CANNOT! GOD CAN! IT IS THE SCRIPTURE DEFINED.

> **...with men this is impossible; but with God all things are possible.**
>
> **Matthew 19:26**

CHAPTER 4

THE MINISTRY OF THE LAYING ON OF HANDS

And when Jesus was come into Peter's
house, he saw his wife's mother laid,
and sick of a fever. And he touched her
hand, and the fever left her: and she
arose, and ministered unto them.

Matthew 8:14,15

A divine touch! One of the ways that healing is ministered is through the laying on of hands.

...they shall lay hands on the sick, and
they shall recover.

Mark 16:18

The Spirit of God reveals to us in His Word that the hands of a believer are consecrated holy unto the Lord.

> **I will therefore that men pray every-where, lifting up holy hands, without wrath and doubting.**
> **1 Timothy 2:8**

The writer of Hebrews states:

> **For we have not an high priest which cannot be touched with the feeling of our infirmities; but was in all points tempted like as we are, yet without sin.**
> **Hebrews 4:15**

You can touch Jesus with your needs. Jesus will touch you and make you whole! Jesus, our high priest, is the fulfillment of every Old Testament priest.

In Israel, once a year, the nation came up to the tabernacle and later, to the temple on the Day of Atonement. One of the symbolic acts of the atonement was the laying on of the priest's hands upon the scapegoat.

Symbolically, the sins of the people were transferred to the goat, which was then driven outside the camp; thus, removing the sins of the people outside the camp!

And Aaron shall lay both his hands upon the head of the live goat, and confess over him all the iniquities of the children of Israel, and all their transgressions in all their sins, putting them upon the head of the goat, and shall send him away by the hand of a fit man into the wilderness: And the goat shall bear upon him all their iniquities unto a land not inhabited: and he shall let go the goat in the wilderness.

Leviticus 16:21,22

God allowed the laying on of hands by the priest to take the sins from the people and to be removed from them, again, by the laying on of hands.

When Jesus laid hands on the sick, they were healed. Christ, as our Substitute, was carrying away those sicknesses in anticipation of His Cross. Jesus carried our sicknesses, as God's scapegoat, He bore them to the Cross.

That it might be fulfilled which was spoken by Esaias the prophet, saying, Himself took our infirmities, and bare our sicknesses.

Matthew 8:17

Jesus fulfilled this prophecy of Isaiah before He went to the Cross! Jesus was healing the sick before Calvary! He was removing diseases from the people on His journey to Calvary. Just as the scapegoat was driven outside the camp, so Christ was crucified outside of the Holy City.

Just as the scapegoat symbolically carried the sins of the people, so Christ carried all sin and sickness upon Himself. Just as the people were left free of all reproach, so we are free from all sin and infirmity. When Jesus laid hands on the sick , He was taking their infirmities. Heaven touched earth and blasted hell. GLORY!

The laying on of hands can impart healing power. There are nine gifts of the Spirit listed in 1 Corinthians 12:1-11. One of these gifts is the *"gifts of healing."*

> **...to another the gifts of healing by the same Spirit.**
> **1 Corinthians 12:9**

The great apostle Paul had tremendous results in getting people to receive healing. He was not a novice.

One of Paul's desires was to help people receive these wonderful, supernatural gifts of God's Spirit. The church in Rome received a letter containing this information:

> **For I long to see you, that I may impart**
> **unto you some spiritual gift, to the end**
> **ye may be established;**
>
> **Romans 1:11**

Spiritual gifts may be imparted or given to believers. Paul even told us one way that those gifts may be given or imparted to that one who believes God's word!

> **Wherefore I put thee in remembrance**
> **that thou stir up the gift of God, which**
> **is in thee by the putting on of my hands.**
>
> **2 Timothy 1:6**

The gift from God that was in Timothy came by Paul putting his hands on him! Spiritual gifts may be given by the laying on of hands. One of those gifts is the *"gifts of healing."* Healing may be given to the one needing that gift by the laying on of hands!

JESUS LAID HANDS ON HIM TWICE

> **And he cometh to Bethsaida; and they**
> **bring a blind man unto him, and be-**
> **sought him to touch him. And he took**
> **the blind man by the hand, and led him**

out of the town; and when he had spit on his eyes, and put his hands upon him, he asked him if he saw ought. And he looked up, and said, I see men as trees, walking. After that he put his hands again upon his eyes, and made him look up: and he was restored, and saw every man clearly.

Mark 8:22-25

The man came to Jesus looking for a touch. Many times in the Scripture, people asked Jesus to pray for them. Here, the man asked for a touch. The Bible says everyone that *"asketh shall receive."*

Jesus never prayed for this blind man! He spit on his eyes. The man was restored so that he could see clearly! Notice, Jesus did not spit again. He laid hands on him again!

Since the Holy Scriptures do not record Jesus praying for the man, and when the miracle was completed, the man saw clearly, God must use the laying on of hands to impart His power into our bodies.

You can receive a miracle through the laying on of hands. God will even work special miracles by the hands of His ministers.

And God wrought special miracles by the hands of Paul: So that from his body were brought unto the sick handkerchiefs or aprons, and the diseases departed from them, and the evil spirits went out of them.

Acts 19:11,12

John G. Lake tells the story of how God used him in bringing a special miracle to a young man through the laying on of hands.

Over in Indiana some years ago was a farmer who was a friend of Brother Fockler and myself. His son had been in South America and had a dreadful case of typhoid fever. He had no proper nursing and as a result, he had developed a great fever sore. It was ten inches in diameter.

The whole abdomen became grown up with proud flesh; one layer on top of another layer, until there were five layers. The nurse had to lift those layers and wash it with an antiseptic to keep the maggots out of it.

When he exposed the body to me to pray for him, I was shocked. I had never seen anything like it before. As I went to pray for him, I spread

49

my fingers out wide, and put my hand on the cursed growth of proud flesh. I prayed God in the Name of Jesus Christ to blast that curse of hell, and burn it up by the power of God. Then I took the train and came back to Chicago. The next day, I received a telegram, saying,

"Lake, the most unusual thing has happened. One hour after you left, the whole print of your hand was burned into that growth a quarter of an inch deep!"

You talk about the voltage from heaven and the power of God! Why there is lightning in the soul of Jesus. The lightnings of Jesus heal men by their flesh; sin dissolves, disease flees when the power of God approaches.

Have faith in God! There is no sin that Christ's blood won't cover. There is no disease He cannot heal. Jesus wants you to be well! Christ is God's plan for ending sickness and disease!

HEALING HANDS

Healing hands reach out to me
from the Cross of Calvary.
Compassion bids my sickness go;

virtue is in that crimson flow!
Life and joy fills my soul,
Healing's song begins to roll.

Happy am I, healed and blessed,
long at last, I'm at rest.
Christ is Healer, of that I'm sure.
He'll be yours, too, friend, open the door!
Sickness and disease will vanish away,
When you experience your healing today!

—Selected

CHAPTER 5
HOW TO KEEP YOUR HEALING

Jesus taught us that it is possible to lose our healing. However, it is God's will for us to keep everything that He gives to us. What must we do, then, to make sure that the enemy does not steal our healing?

It is possible to lose what God gives you. This is true of every blessing that He makes available to us. Jesus healed a crippled man at the pool of Bethesda. Later, when He saw him at the temple, He warned the man to stay free from sin now that he was healed, or a worse thing could come on him (John 5:14).

The Bible says that, *"Discretion shall preserve thee, understanding shall KEEP thee:" (Proverbs 2:11).* We need to have an understanding of how to keep what the Lord gives us. This is especially true of the healing that we may receive in our minds and bodies.

I prayed for a deaf woman in Indiana, some years ago. She had not heard out of either ear for over twenty years. Her son was a minister friend of mine and had asked me to pray for his mother when I was in her city.

Her other son brought her to the meeting, and I prayed for her at the end of the service. Instantly, both of her ears came open and she could hear the ticking of a watch in both ears. The people praised God for it was a wonderful miracle.

They went out to go home as I began to pray for others. Five minutes later, the back door opened and her son motioned for me to come to the back of the church.

When I went back, he said, "Mom, locked herself in the car." He told me that she was mad. When I asked him why, he told me that both of her ears had closed, and she was deaf again.

He told me that as they were leaving the church he said to his mother, "Isn't it great that Jesus healed you?"

"I hope it lasts," she replied. She could not keep her healing for more than five minutes.

The more valuable your blessing, the more the devil will try to steal it from you.

The Bible teaches us that God *"Will keep the feet of His saints."* (1 Samuel 2:9).

The Scriptures also declare, *"But the Lord is faithful,*

who shall stablish you, and keep you from evil." (2 Thessalonians 3:3).

WE ARE KEPT BY GOD'S WORD

So then faith cometh by hearing, and hearing by the Word of God.

Romans 10:17

You need to read His Word to strengthen your faith. Doubt will rob you of healing every time. Find a promise from the Bible that has to do with what you need, and build your faith on that promise.

The faith that comes from these promises puts you in touch with Him, and gives you the ability to receive and keep the very thing that you have needed.

We are kept by the HEARD WORD! Jesus spoke of the sower who sowed the seed in four kinds of ground. He said that the seed was the Word of God. You are God's good ground! Jesus said:

> **But that on the good ground are they, which in an honest and good heart, having heard the word, KEEP it, and bring forth fruit with patients.**
>
> **Luke 8:15**

That is why I believe that it is vitally important to go to a church where the healing word is sown. You cannot expect to keep your healing or anything God gives you if you attend a church that does not believe that the Lord heals today, or that he will heal everyone who comes to Him in faith believing.

You keep your healing by getting in an atmosphere of faith created by hearing the Word.

WE ARE KEPT BY OUR CONFESSION

If you want to keep your healing, then you must resist the devil. The devil does not want us to learn the life of faith or the biblical laws that govern it.

The enemy constantly seeks to make us fearful and cause us to doubt. Many times over the years I've seen the devil try to bring the old symptoms back on someone after they have been healed.

> **Submit yourselves therefore to God. Resist the devil and HE WILL FLEE FROM YOU.**
>
> **James 4:7**

It has been said that we rise or fall according to the level of our confession. That woman in Indiana allowed her words to reopen the door to deafness, and I am sure to bitterness as well. We must learn to talk back to the devil. I love to shout that verse in Isaiah:

> **But he was wounded for our transgressions, he was bruised for our iniquities: the chastisement of our peace was upon him; and with his stripes WE ARE HEALED.**
>
> **Isaiah 53:5**

WE ARE KEPT BY OUR PRAISE

We need to learn how to praise God by faith before and after we receive our healing. Praise Him before you see it or feel it. Then, praise Him for what He has done after you receive it.

> **REJOICE in the Lord always: and again I say, REJOICE. Let your moderation be known unto all men, the Lord is at hand. Be careful for nothing; but in everything by prayer and supplication with THANKSGIVING let your requests be made known unto God. And the peace of God, which passeth all understand-**

ing, shall KEEP your hearts and minds
through Christ Jesus.

Philippians 4:4-7

Your praise can also make you whole. The things that
the disease or sickness may have taken from your mind
and body will be restored as you praise the Lord for His
wonderful works.

DOWNLOAD OUR APP.

Search "Ted Shuttlesworth" in the Apple App Store or the Google Play Store.

DO YOU NEED PRAYER?

Call us today: 1-888-323-2484

Visit us online: www.tedshuttlesworth.com

TED SHUTTLESWORTH

The Camels
Are Coming

Introduction to the
Gifts of the Spirit
Volume 1

THE CAMELS ARE COMING

Your success in life is birthed out of your understanding of Spiritual Gifts. Their importance is critical in the end times as we deal with deception and evil.

This book is an examination of the existence and purpose of the Gifts of the Spirit. There are three Gifts that can bring a life-changing word from God. There are three Gifts that can bring healing and help for the spirit, soul, and body. There are three gifts that can reveal God's design and plan past, present, and future.

shop.tedshuttlesworth.com

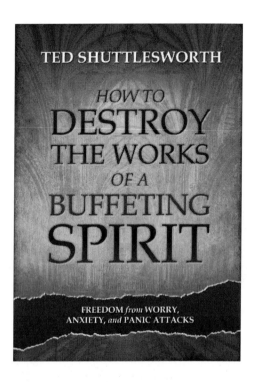

TED SHUTTLESWORTH

HOW TO
DESTROY
THE WORKS
OF A
BUFFETING
SPIRIT

FREEDOM *from* WORRY, ANXIETY, *and* PANIC ATTACKS

HOW TO DESTROY THE WORKS OF A BUFFETING SPIRIT

Today we are witnessing unrest and trouble which are affecting the nations of the world. There are many who are fearful because of the uncertainty of the times.

Anxiety disorders are the most common mental illness in the United States affecting 40 million adults 18 years of age and older according to the National Institute of Mental Health.

There are many people who are managing anxiety with medications, psychiatrists, and even hypnosis. What if these attacks were being caused by demon spirits? Learn what the Bible has to say about how to be free from worry, fear, anxiety, and panic attacks!

shop.tedshuttlesworth.com

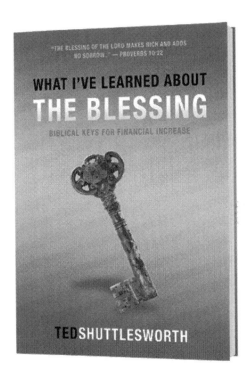

"THE BLESSING OF THE LORD MAKES RICH AND ADDS NO SORROW." — PROVERBS 10:22

WHAT I'VE LEARNED ABOUT
THE BLESSING

BIBLICAL KEYS FOR FINANCIAL INCREASE

TEDSHUTTLESWORTH

WHAT I'VE LEARNED ABOUT THE BLESSING

God's Blessing will take you from financial failure to a good life. Throughout the years I have proven that the biblical principles of increase work.

I gave God one dollar when I was eighteen, and He gave me a ministry to touch the World. I have learned that The Blessing is greater than the curse and the Lord cannot fail.

You can be the one that changes your family's financial future. There are many of God's Children who are living far below their potential. When you understand the connection between prosperity and the winning of lost souls and faithfully operate in these Biblical principles then you can expect to receive God's Blessing.

shop.tedshuttlesworth.com

Made in the USA
Columbia, SC
31 October 2021